Knit Baby Animal Patterns

Amigurumi Animals

COMPLETE GUIDE TO KNIT DOLL TECHNIQUES MADE EASY

Volume 2

Patterns by Cherix Knit a Dream

Edit by

Publish by

ISBN: 9798364507334

Content

My little bunny

Amy

Knitting pattern by Cheryx

The seventeenth dream

Needles

- A pair of 2.5mm straight knitting needles

Materials

- Toy filling (less than 50g)
- Tapestry needle
- Scissors
- Sewing pins
- 2 Holders
- 2 beads - for the eyes (4 mm)
- 1 button (size 10 mm)

Yarns

Less than 50g in each colour:

- Nako Paris

   Gray 1690

- Jeans - Yarn Art

  ⚪ White 01

  ⚫ Black 53

- DMC Woolly

  🟣 Light pink 41

  🟣 Pink 45

  🟣 Purple 62

Notes

- **Finished size:** The finished bunny is 20cm tall

- **Gauge:** 26 sts and 34 rows = 4" [10 cm] in stockinette stitch. Don't worry too much about tension for this pattern.

- **Work flat:** All pieces are knitted flat

- **Casting on:** Unless otherwise specified, I prefer to use the long tail cast on for all pieces.

- **Sewing seams:** Use Mattress Stitch and Whip Stitch to sew the seams.

- **Safety:** If you are making these toys to give to a child, please consider your choice of toy eyes carefully, and ensure you have no loose parts (loose threads, buttons, etc) which can be potential.

Abbreviations

K	Knit
P	Purl
Kfb	*Increase:* Knit into the front and back of the next stitch
K2tog	*Decrease:* Knit two stitches together
SSK	*Decrease:* Slip a stitch (as if to knit it) to the right needle, slip a second stitch in the same way, slip both stitches together back to the left needle and knit together through the back loops.
KRL	*Increase:* With your right needle, come from behind and scoop up the right loop of the "V" stitch just below the one on your left needle. Lift this loop up into your left needle. Knit the loop.
KLL	*Increase:* After working a knit stitch, identify the stitch 2 rows below the one on your right needle. With your left needle, come from behind to scoop up the left loop of this stitch. This loop on the left needle is the new stitch. Insert the right needle tip through the back loop and knit.
st(s)	Stitch(es)
St st	**Stockinette Stitch: K**nit all stitches on right side rows, purl all stitches on wrong side rows.
(...sts)	The number in round brackets at the end of the instruction indicates the number of stitches after working the row.
[...]	Repeat the sequence between the square brackets by the number indicated.

• •

Knitting Pattern

Head (Knit 1 piece)

Cast on 7 stitches with the gray yarn.

Row 1: KFB x7   (14 sts)

Row 2: P14   (14 sts)

Row 3: K1, [KRL, K1] x3, KRL, K1, KFB , K2, KFB, K1, KLL, [K1, KLL] x3, K1   (24 sts)

Row 4: P24   (24 sts)

Row 5: K1, [K1, KRL] x7, K8, [KLL, K1] x7, K1   (38 sts)

Row 6: P38   (38 sts)

Row 7: K1, [K2, KRL] x7, K8 , [KLL, K2] x7, K1   (52 sts)

Row 8 – Row 22: St st   (52 sts)

Using 2 ends of different color yarn to marker. (I've used green yarn to illustrate). Where 2 ends of the green yarn come out, we will sew the ears to the head later.

Row 23: K16, place marker by one end of the green yarn *(Fig. 1)*, K20, place marker by the other end of yarn *(Fig. 2)*, K16 *(Fig. 3)*   (52 sts)

Fig. 1   Fig. 2   Fig. 3

Row 24 – Row 32: St st   (52 sts)

Using 2 ends of different color yarn to marker. (I've used yellow yarn to illustrate). Where 2 ends of the yellow yarn come out, we will attach the eyes to the head later.

Row 33: K1, K2tog x8, place marker by one end of the yellow yarn, K2tog x3, K6, K2tog x3, place marker by the other end of yarn, K2tog x8, K1 *(Fig. 4)*   (30 sts)

Row 34: P30   (30 sts)

Row 35: K11, SSK, K4, K2tog, K11   (28 sts)

Row 36: P28   (28 sts)

Row 37: K1, K2tog x6, K2, K2tog x6, K1   (16 sts)

Fig. 4

Row 38: P16   (16 sts)

Row 39: K5, K2tog, K2, K2tog, K5   (14 sts)

Row 40: P14   (14 sts)

Row 41: K2tog x7   (7 sts)

Leave a long tail for sewing, then cut off the yarn.

Thread this tail through remaining stitches and pull up tightly.

Body (Knit 1 piece)

Cast on 20 stitches with the gray yarn (leave a long tail for sewing).

Row 1: K20   (20 sts)

Row 2: P20   (20 sts)

Row 3: K1, [K3, KLL] x6, K1   (26 sts)

Row 4 – Row 8: St st   (26 sts)

Row 9: K1, [K4, KLL] x6, K1   (32 sts)

Row 10 – Row 14: St st   (32 sts)

Row 15: K1, [K5, KLL] x6, K1   (38 sts)

Row 16 – Row 20: St st   (38 sts)

Row 21: K1, [K6, KLL] x6, K1   (44 sts)

Row 22 – Row 24: St st   (44 sts)

Cut off the gray yarn, continue knitting with the white yarn.

Row 25: K44   (44 sts)

Row 26 (Wrong side): K44   (44 sts)

Row 27: K1, [K7, KLL] x6, K1   (50 sts)

Row 28: P50   (50 sts)

Row 29 – Row 38: St st   (50 sts)

Row 39: Cast off 3 stitches (remaining 46 stitches on the left needle to work), K19, cast off 4 stitches (remaining 22 stitches on the left needle to work), K19, cast off remaining stitches *(Fig. 5)* (40 sts)

We have 40 stitches to knit the legs. Transfer 20 stitches on the left to a holder to knit later. We'll use white yarn to continue knitting 20 stitches on the right first (Fig. 6).

Fig. 5   *Fig. 6*

Row 1: K20 (20 sts)

Row 2: P20 (20 sts)

Cut off the white yarn, continue knitting with the gray yarn.

Row 3: K1, [K4, K2tog] x3, K1 (17 sts)

Row 4 – Row 8: St st (17 sts)

Row 9: K1, [K3, K2tog] x3, K1 (14 sts)

Row 10 – Row 14: St st (14 sts)

Row 15: K1, [K4, K2tog] x2, K1 (12 sts)

Row 16 – Row 18: St st (12 sts)

Cut off the gray yarn, continue knitting with the white yarn.

Row 19: K12 (12 sts)

Row 20 (Wrong side): K12 (12 sts)

Row 21: K12 (12 sts)

Row 22: P12 (12 sts)

Cut off the white yarn, continue knitting with the black yarn.

Row 23: K12 (12 sts)

Row 24 (Wrong side): K4, cast on 11 stitches, K8 (23 sts)

Row 25: K13, KFB, K9 (24 sts)

Row 26: P24 (24 sts)

Row 27: K13, KLL, K2, KRL, K9 (26 sts)

Row 28: P26 (26 sts)

Row 29: K13, KLL, K4, KRL, K9 (28 sts)

Row 30: P28 (28 sts)

Row 31: K13, KLL, K6, KRL, K9 (30 sts)

Row 32: P30 (30 sts)

Row 33: K30 (30 sts)

Row 34 (Wrong side): K30 (30 sts)

Row 35: K1, K2tog, [K2, K2tog] x3, [K2tog, K2] x3, K2tog, K1 (22 sts)

Row 36: P22 (22 sts)

Row 37: K2tog, [K1, K2tog] x3, [K2tog, K1] x3, K2tog (14 sts)

Row 38: Cast off

Cut off the yarn *(Fig. 7)*.

Now, We'll use white yarn to continue knitting 20 stitches on the holder (Fig. 8).

Fig. 7   *Fig. 8*

Row 1 – Row 22: Repeat **Row 1 – Row 22** of the first leg.

Cut off the white yarn, continue knitting with the black yarn.

Row 23: K12 (12 sts)

Row 24 (Wrong side): K8, cast on 11 stitches, K4 (23 sts)

Row 25: K9, KFB, K13 (24 sts)

Row 26: P24 (24 sts)

Row 27: K9, KLL, K2, KRL, K13 (26 sts)

Row 28: P26 (26 sts)

Row 29: K9, KLL, K4, KRL, K13 (28 sts)

Row 30: P28 (28 sts)

Row 31: K9, KLL, K6, KRL, K13 (30 sts)

Row 32: P30 (30 sts)

Row 33: K30 (30 sts)

Row 34 (Wrong side): K30 (30 sts)

Row 35: K1, K2tog, [K2, K2tog] x3, [K2tog, K2] x3, K2tog, K1 (22 sts)

Row 36: P22   (22 sts)

Row 37: K2tog, [K1, K2tog] x3, [K2tog, K1] x3, K2tog   (14 sts)

Row 38: Cast off

Cut off the yarn.

Arms (Knit 2 pieces)

Cast on 8 stitches with the gray yarn (leave a long tail for sewing).

Row 1: K8   (8 sts)

Row 2: P8   (8 sts)

Row 3 – Row 4: St st   (8 sts)

Row 5: K1, [K2, KLL] x3, K1   (11 sts)

Row 6 – Row 10: St st   (11 sts)

Row 11: K1, [K3, KLL] x3, K1   (14 sts)

Row 12 – Row 16: St st   (14 sts)

Row 17: K1, [K4, KLL] x3, K1   (17 sts)

Row 18 – Row 30: St st   (17 sts)

Row 31: K1, K2tog, K4, SSK, K2tog, K3, SSK, K1   (13 sts)

Row 32: P13   (13 sts)

Row 33: K1, K2tog, K2, SSK, K2tog, K1, SSK, K1   (9 sts)

Row 34: P9   (9 sts)

Row 35: K1, [K2tog, SSK] x2   (5 sts)

Leave a long tail for sewing, then cut off the yarn.

Thread this tail through remaining stitches and pull up tightly.

Ears (Knit 2 pieces)

Cast on 14 stitches with the gray yarn (leave a long tail for sewing).

Row 1: K14   (14 sts)

Row 2: P14   (14 sts)

Row 3 – Row 6: St st   (14 sts)

Row 7: K1, [K3, KLL] x4, K1   (18 sts)

Row 8 – Row 14: St st   (18 sts)

Row 15: K1, [K4, KLL] x4, K1   (22 sts)

Row 16 – Row 22: St st   (22 sts)

Row 23: K1, [K5, KLL] x4, K1   (26 sts)

Row 24 – Row 30: St st   (26 sts)

Row 31: K1, [K6, KLL] x4, K1   (30 sts)

Row 32 – Row 36: St st   (30 sts)

Row 37: K1, [K7, KLL] x4, K1   (34 sts)

Row 38 – Row 58: St st   (34 sts)

Row 59: K2, [K3, K2tog] x6, K2   (28 sts)

Row 60: P28   (28 sts)

Row 61: K2, [K2, K2tog] x6, K2   (22 sts)

Row 62: P22   (22 sts)

Row 63: K2, [K1, K2tog] x6, K2   (16 sts)

Row 64: P16   (16 sts)

Row 65: K2tog x8   (8 sts)

Leave a long tail for sewing, then cut off the yarn.

Thread this tail through remaining stitches and pull up tightly.

Dress (Knit 1 piece)

Cast on 26 stitches with the light pink yarn (leave a long tail).

Row 1: P26   (26 sts)

Row 2: K4, yo, K1, yo, K3, yo, K1, yo, K8, yo, K1, yo, K3, yo, K1, yo, K4   (34 sts)

Row 3: P34   (34 sts)

Row 4: K5, yo, K1, yo, K5, yo, K1, yo, K10, yo, K1, yo, K5, yo, K1, yo, K5   (42 sts)

Row 5: P42   (42 sts)

Row 6: K6, yo, K1, yo, K7, yo, K1, yo, K12, yo, K1, yo, K7, yo, K1, yo, K6   (50 sts)

Row 7: P50   (50 sts)

Row 8: K7, yo, K1, yo, K9, yo, K1, yo, K14, yo, K1, yo, K9, yo, K1, yo, K7   (58 sts)

Row 9: P58   (58 sts)

Row 10: K8, yo, K1, yo, K11, yo, K1, yo, K16, yo, K1, yo, K11, yo, K1, yo, K8   (66 sts)

Row 11: P66   (66 sts)

Row 12: K9, yo, K1, yo, K13, yo, K1, yo, K18, yo, K1, yo, K13, yo, K1, yo, K9   (74 sts)

Row 13: P74   (74 sts)

Row 14: K12 *(Fig. 9)*, transfer the 12 stitches to the first holder *(Fig.10)*, continue knitting K26 *(Fig. 11)*, transfer the 12 stitches to the second holder *(Fig. 12)*, continue knitting K12 *(Fig. 13)*   (50 sts)

Row 15: P50   (50 sts)

Fig. 9

Fig. 10

Fig. 11

Fig. 12

Fig. 13

Cut off the light pink yarn, continue knitting with the pink yarn.

Row 16: K50   (50 sts)

Row 17: P50   (50 sts)

Cut off the pink yarn, continue knitting with the light pink yarn.

Row 18: K50   (50 sts)

Row 19: P1, [P2, K1] x16, P1   (50 sts)

Row 20: K1, [P1, KRL, K2] x16, K1   (66 sts)

Row 21: P1, [P3, K1] x16, P1   (66 sts)

Row 22: K1, [P1, KRL, K3] x16, K1   (82 sts)

Row 23 – Row 43: St st   (82 sts)

Cut off the light pink yarn, continue knitting with the pink yarn.

Row 44: K82   (82 sts)

Row 45 (Wrong side): K82   (82 sts)

Cut off the pink yarn, continue knitting with the purple yarn.

Row 46: K82   (82 sts)

Row 47: P82   (82 sts)

Cut off the purple yarn, continue knitting with the pink yarn.

Row 48: K82   (82 sts)

Row 49: K82   (82 sts)

Cut off the pink yarn, continue knitting with the light pink yarn.

Row 50: K1, [K4, slip 1 stitch] x16, K1   (82 sts)

Row 51: K1, [slip 1 stitch, K4] x16, K1   (82 sts)

Row 52: K1, [K4, slip 1 stitch] x16, K1   (82 sts)

Row 53: Cast off

Cut off the yarn *(Fig. 14)*.

Fig. 14

We will work with the stitches on holders: Transfer the stitches to knitting needle, then cast off with the pink yarn *(Fig. 15 - Fig. 17)*.

Fig. 15   *Fig. 16*   *Fig. 17*

Sew & Make up

*You can see the Tutorial videos of my knitting patterns on **Cheryx.com***

(Cheryx.com > Tips & Tutorials > Tutorial videos)

HOME   PATTERNS   FREE PATTERNS   TIPS & TUTORIALS   FAQs   CONTATT

Home > Tips & Tutorials

🐻 Toy making techniques

 Tutorial videos

🧶 Needles & yarns

✂ Seams & Finishing

🔘 Other

Christmas reindeer Christopher – Tutorial videos

This is the tutorial video of knitting pattern "The friendly reindeer Christopher"

Mr.Pumpkin – Tutorial videos

This is the tutorial video of knitting pattern "The midnight guest Mr.Pumpkin"

Wooden doll Pinocchio – Tutorial videos

These are the tutorial videos of knitting pattern "My wooden doll Pinocchio"

Legs & Body

Using the tapestry needle to thread the cast on tail, sewing 2 side edges together (sewing from A to B). Adding stuffing as you sew. *(Fig. 18)*

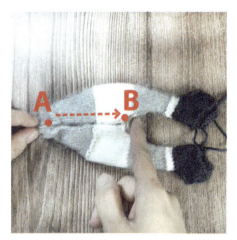

Fig. 18

Using the cast off tail of the shoe to sew form C to D with Whip Stitch *(Fig. 19)*. Repeat with the second shoe. Then, sewing from E to F with Mattress Stitch *(Fig. 20)*. Adding stuffing as you sew.

Fig. 19

Fig. 20

We will use the black yarn to sew the opening in the upper part of the shoes *(Fig. 21 - Fig. 23)*

Fig. 21

Fig. 22

Fig. 23

Arms

We'll fold the arm and use the tapestry needle with cast off tail to sew the side edges together with help of the Mattress Stitch. Halfway along the seam, we will stop and lightly stuff the arm, leaving the top of arm unstuffed so it stays floppy.

Continue sewing to the cast on edge, tie off 2 tails together. Repeat with the second arm.

Ears

We'll fold the ear and use the tapestry needle with cast off tail to sew the side edges together with help of the Mattress Stitch. Don't add stuffing.

Head

If you use the toy eyes with thread end and washer buckle (plastic washers) *(Fig. 24)*, you'll attach the eyes first before you sew the head.

Attaching the eyes to the place where we marked earlier (2 ends of yellow yarn) . Then secure it in place with the eye backs *(Fig. 25 - Fig. 26)*.

Fig. 24   *Fig. 25*   *Fig. 26*

Using the tapestry needle with cast off tail to sew the side edges together. Adding stuffing as you sew. On the open end, thread your yarn through the loops of the cast on stitches and pull it together to close the opening (I've used red to illustrate) *(Fig. 27 - Fig. 28)*.

When finished, we will tie off all the tails together and poke them into body to hide.

Fig. 27   *Fig. 28*

Eyes & Nose

(You can see the Tutorial Video of this step on Cheryx.com > Tips & Tutorials > Tutorial Videos)

Using black yarn to embroider the eyes *(Fig. 29 - Fig. 34)*.

Fig. 29   Fig. 30   Fig. 31

Fig. 32   Fig. 33   Fig. 34

Using black yarn to embroider the nose and the eyebrows *(Fig. 35 - Fig. 37)*. Then, using the pink yarn to make up the nose *(Fig. 38 - Fig. 39)*.

Fig. 35   Fig. 36   Fig. 37

Fig. 38   Fig. 39

Sew the ears into the head

Using the sewing pins to adjust the ears to the place where we marked earlier (2 ends of green yarn) *(Fig. 40 - Fig. 41)*.

Fig. 40   *Fig. 41*

Then using a long tail to attact the ears into the head (sewing through a stitch of the head *(Fig. 42)* and then through a stitch of the ear *(Fig. 43)*). When finished, hiding all tails inside the head *(Fig. 44)*.

Fig. 42   *Fig. 43*   *Fig. 44*

Using pink yarn to embroider cheeks *(Fig. 45 - Fig. 48)*.

Fig. 45   *Fig. 46*   *Fig. 47*   *Fig. 48*

Sew the head into the body

It's time to attach the finished head to the finished body. We'll adjust the head with sewing pins to the body *(Fig. 49)*.

Thread the tapestry needle with one of the long tails from the neck and use it to sew the body and head together (Sewing through a stitch of the head *(Fig. 50)* and then through a stitch on the cast off edge of the neck *(Fig. 51)*.

While attaching them, stuff the neck as tightly as you can, so that the head can stay up and not droop.

When finished, we will tie off all the tails together and poke them into body to hide.

Fig. 49	Fig. 50	Fig. 51

Sew the arms into the body

Using the sewing pins to adjust the arms to the body. Then using a long tail to sew the arms into the body.

When finished, hiding all tails inside the body *(Fig. 52)*.

Fig. 52

Embroider the flowers on the dress

(You can see the Tutorial Video of this step on Cheryx.com > Tips & Tutorials > Tutorial Videos)

Using the pink, purple, white and green yarn to embroider the flowers on the dress as shown in the figures *(Fig. 53 - Fig. 58)*.

How to embroider the "Spider Web Rose Stitch":

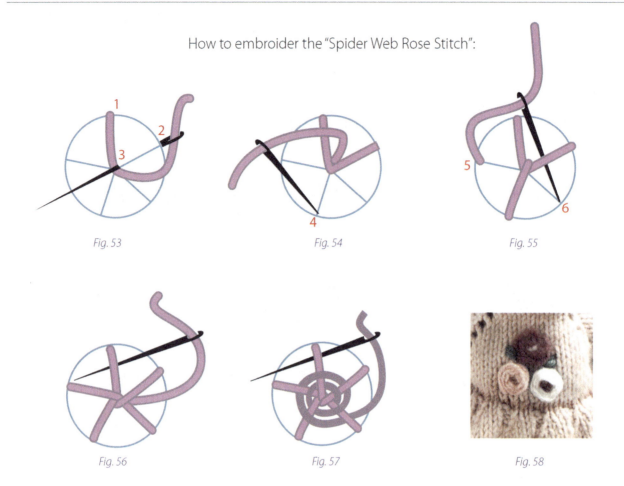

Fig. 53

Fig. 54

Fig. 55

Fig. 56

Fig. 57

Fig. 58

Sew the dress

Thread the tapestry needle with cast off long tail of dress to sew form G to H *(Fig. 59)*.

Sewing a small button into the dress. Then, using cast on long tail to make a buttonhole *(Fig. 60 - Fig. 61)*.

Fig. 59

Fig. 60

Fig. 61

Knitting pattern of the mini bunny

Head & Body (Knit 1 piece)

Cast on 8 stitches with white yarn.

Row 1: KFB x8		(16 sts)
Row 2: P16		(16 sts)
Row 3: [K3, KFB] x4		(20 sts)
Row 4 – Row 14: St st		(20 sts)
Row 15: K2tog x10		(10 sts)
Row 16: P10		(10 sts)
Row 17: KFB x 10		(20 sts)
Row 18: P20		(20 sts)
Row 19 – Row 24: St st		(20 sts)
Row 25: K2tog x 10		(10 sts)
Row 26: P10		(10 sts)
Row 27: K2tog x5		(5 sts)

Leaving a long tail for sewing, then cut off the yarn.

Thread this tail through remaining stitches and pull up tightly.

Arms & Legs (Knit 4 pieces)

Cast on 6 stitches with white yarn.

Row 1: K6	(6 sts)
Row 2: P6	(6 sts)
Row 3 – Row 14: St st	(6 sts)
Row 15: K2tog x3	(3 sts)

Leaving a long tail for sewing, then cut off the yarn.

Thread this tail through remaining stitches and pull up tightly.

Ears (Knit 2 pieces)

Cast on 4 stitches with white yarn.

Row 1: K4 (4 sts)

Row 2: P4 (4 sts)

Row 3 – Row 8: St st (4 sts)

Row 9: K1, KRL, K2, KLL, K1 (6 sts)

Row 10 – Row 18: St st (6 sts)

Row 19: K1, KRL, K4, KLL, K1 (8 sts)

Row 20 – Row 24: St st (8 sts)

Row 25: K1, K2topg, K2, K2tog, K1 (6 sts)

Row 26: P6 (6 sts)

Row 27: K1, K2tog x2, K1 (4 sts)

Row 28: P4 (4 sts)

Row 29: K2tog x2 (2 sts)

Leaving a long tail for sewing, then cut off the yarn.

Thread this tail through remaining stitches and pull up tightly.

. . . .

Sew & Make up

Head and body

Using the white yarn (about 10 inch) and the tapestry needle to thread this yarn through a few stitches in Row 15 (I've used red to illustrate) *(Fig. 62)*.

Using the tapestry needle with cast off tail to sew the side edges together right up to the cast on edge, thread your yarn through the loops of the cast on stitches and pull it together to close the opening. Adding stuffing as you sew.

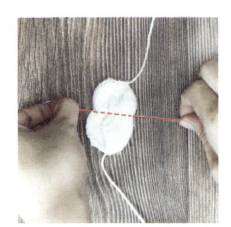

Fig. 62

To shape the neck, pull up gathers tightly, then we will tie off 2 tails together and poke them inside body to hide.

Arms & legs

Sewing the side edges together with Whip Stitch, don't add stuffing.

Then, using the sewing pins to adjust the arms and legs to the body *(Fig. 63)* and sewing them in place.

Fig. 63

Ears

Using the sewing pins to adjust the ears to the head. Then using a long tail to sew it in place *(Fig. 64)*.

Embroider the eyes & nose

Using black yarn to embroider the eyes and nose *(Fig. 64)*.

Fig. 64

Dear Customer

I am on emerging editor and, with the sales made by the book, I can continue my studies to publish other books on the subject. I would appreciate on honest review from you.

Also, please if you notice any mistakes or missing information, feel free to contact me at this e-mail address: wwwanacraft@gmail.com
Thank you for your support

Write to us to get extra free content for you

The friendly reindeer

Christopher

• Knitting pattern by Cheryx •

The sixteenth dream

Needles

- Two pairs of 2.25mm (US 1) straight knitting needles

Materials

- Toy filling (less than 50g)
- Tapestry needle
- Scissors
- Sewing pins
- 1 Holder needle
- 2 beads - for the eyes (4 mm)
- 4 buttons (size 10 mm)

Yarns

Less than 50g in each colour:

- Susan

  - Light beige 18
  - Brown 61
  - Light brown 26
  - Red 24
  - Green 32
  - Light gray 11
  - Drak gray 36

Notes

- **Finished size:** The finished reindeer is 33cm tall

- **Gauge:** 26 sts and 34 rows = 4" [10 cm] in stockinette stitch. Don't worry too much about tension for this pattern.

- **Work flat:** All pieces are knitted flat

- **Casting on:** Unless otherwise specified, I prefer to use the long tail cast on for all pieces.

- **Sewing seams:** Use Mattress Stitch and Whip Stitch to sew the seams.

- **Safety:** If you are making these toys to give to a child, please consider your choice of toy eyes carefully, and ensure you have no loose parts (loose threads, buttons, etc) which can be potential.

ABBREVIATIONS

K	Knit
P	Purl
Kfb	*Increase:* Knit into the front and back of the next stitch
K2tog	*Decrease:* Knit two stitches together
P2tog	*Decrease:* Purl two stitches together
SSK	*Decrease:* Slip a stitch (as if to knit it) to the right needle, slip a second stitch in the same way, slip both stitches together back to the left needle and knit together through the back loops.
KRL	*Increase:* With your right needle, come from behind and scoop up the right loop of the "V" stitch just below the one on your left needle. Lift this loop up into your left needle. Knit the loop.
KLL	*Increase:* After working a knit stitch, identify the stitch 2 rows below the one on your right needle. With your left needle, come from behind to scoop up the left loop of this stitch. This loop on the left needle is the new stitch. Insert the right needle tip through the back loop and knit.
st(s)	Stitch(es)
St st	Stockinette Stitch: Knit all stitches on right side rows, purl all stitches on wrong side rows.
(...sts)	The number in round brackets at the end of the instruction indicates the number of stitches after working the row.
[...]	Repeat the sequence between the square brackets by the number indicated.

KNITTING PATTERN

LEGS & BODY

The first leg:

Cast on 16 stitches in red, leaving a long tail for sewing.

Row 1: K16   (16 sts)

Row 2: P16   (16 sts)

Row 3 – Row 5: St st   (16 sts)

Row 6 (Wrong side): K16   (16 sts)

Cut off the red yarn, continue knitting with the light beige yarn.

Row 7: K16   (16 sts)

Row 8 – Row 12: St st   (16 sts)

Row 13: K1, [K7, KLL] x2, K1   (18 sts)

Row 14 – Row 24: St st   (18 sts)

Row 25: K1, [K8, KLL] x2, K1   (20 sts)

Row 26 – Row 34: St st   (20 sts)

Cut off the light beige yarn, continue knitting with the brown.

Row 35: K1, [K9, KLL] x2, K1   (22 sts)

Row 36 – Row 40: St st   (22 sts)

Fig. 1

Cut off the yarn, then we'll tranfer 22 stitches to the holder needle to knit later. (Fig. 1)

The second leg:

Repeat Row 1 – Row 40 of the first leg. But don't cut off the yarn, we'll continue knitting row 41.

Row 41: Cast on 3 stitches *(Fig. 2)*, K25, cast on 5 stitches *(Fig. 3)*, continue knitting K22 (22 stitches of the first leg *(Fig. 4)*), cast on 3 stitches *(Fig. 5)* (55 sts)

Fig. 2   Fig. 3   Fig. 4   Fig. 5

Row 42: P55   (55 sts)

Row 43 – Row 66: St st   (55 sts)

Cut off the brown yarn, continue knitting with the light gray.

Row 67: K2, [K11, K2tog] x4, K1   (51 sts)

Row 68 (Wrong side): K51   (51 sts)

Row 69 – Row 76: St st   (51 sts)

Row 77: K2, [K10, K2tog] x4, K1   (47 sts)

Row 78 – Row 86: St st   (47 sts)

Row 87: K2, [K9, K2tog] x4, K1   (43 sts)

Row 88 – Row 96: St st   (43 sts)

Row 97: K2, [K8, K2tog] x4, K1   (39 sts)

Row 98 – Row 106: St st   (39 sts)

Row 107: K2, [K7, K2tog] x4, K1   (35 sts)

Row 108: P35   (35 sts)

Row 109: K35   (35 sts)

Row 110 (Wrong side): K35   (35 sts)

Cut off the light gray yarn, continue knitting with the light beige.

Row 111: [K5, K2tog] x5   (30 sts)

Row 112: P30   (30 sts)

We have 30 stitches on the left knitting neddle. Transfer 15 stitches on the left to a holder to knit later.

We'll knit 15 stitches on the right first. (Fig. 6)

Row 113: K10, K2tog x2, K1   (13 sts)

Row 114: P13   (13 sts)

Row 115: K8, K2tog x2, K1   (11 sts)

Row 116: P11   (11 sts)

Row 117: K6, K2tog x2, K1   (9 sts)

Row 118: P9   (9 sts)

Row 119: K4, K2tog x2, K1   (7 sts)

Row 120: P7   (7 sts)

Row 121: K4, K2tog, K1   (6 sts)

Fig. 6

Row 122: P6   (6 sts)

Row 123: K3, K2tog, K1   (5 sts)

Row 124: P5   (5 sts)

Row 125: K2, K2tog, K1   (4 sts)

Row 126: P4   (4 sts)

Row 127: K1, K2tog, K1   (3 sts)

Row 128: P3   (3 sts)

Row 129: Cast off

Then, we'll use the light beige yarn to continue knitting 15 stitches on holder needle. *(Fig. 7 - Fig. 8)*

Fig. 7

Fig. 8

Row 1: K1, SSK x2, K10   (13 sts)

Row 2: P13   (13 sts)

Row 3: K1, SSK x2, K8   (11 sts)

Row 4: P11   (11 sts)

Row 5: K1, SSK x2, K6   (9 sts)

Row 6: P9   (9 sts)

Row 7: K1, SSK x2, K4   (7 sts)

Row 8: P7   (7 sts)

Row 9: K1, SSK, K4   (6 sts)

Row 10: P6   (6 sts)

Row 11: K1, SSK, K3   (5 sts)

Row 12: P5   (5 sts)

Row 13: K1, SSK, K2   (4 sts)

Row 14: P4   (4 sts)

Row 15: K1, SSK, K1   (3 sts)

Row 16: P3   (3 sts)

Row 17: Cast off. *(Fig. 9 - Fig. 10)*

Fig. 9   Fig. 10

ARMS (Make 2)

Cast on 12 stitches in light gray, leaving a long tail for sewing.

Row 1: K12   (12 sts)

Row 2: P12   (12 sts)

Row 3: K12   (12 sts)

Row 4: P12   (12 sts)

Cut off the light gray yarn, continue knitting with the dark gray.

Row 5: K1, KRL, K10, KLL, K1   (14 sts)

Row 6: P14   (14 sts)

Cut off the dark gray yarn, continue knitting with the light gray.

Row 7 – Row 10: St st   (14 sts)

Cut off the light gray yarn, continue knitting with the dark gray.

Row 11 – Row 12: St st   (14 sts)

Cut off the dark gray yarn, continue knitting with the light gray.

Row 13 – Row 14: St st   (14 sts)

Row 15: K1, KRL, K12, KLL, K1   (16 sts)

Row 16: P16   (16 sts)

Cut off the light gray yarn, continue knitting with the dark gray.

Row 17 – Row 18: St st   (16 sts)

Cut off the dark gray yarn, continue knitting with the light gray.

Row 19 – Row 22: St st   (16 sts)

Cut off the light gray yarn, continue knitting with the dark gray.

Row 23 – Row 24: St st   (16 sts)

Cut off the dark gray yarn, continue knitting with the light gray.

Row 25: K1, KRL, K14, KLL, K1   (18 sts)

Row 26 – Row 28: St st   (18 sts)

Cut off the light gray yarn, continue knitting with the dark gray.

Row 29 – Row 30: St st   (18 sts)

Cut off the dark gray yarn, continue knitting with the light gray.

Row 31 – Row 34: St st   (18 sts)

Cut off the light gray yarn, continue knitting with the dark gray.

Row 35 – Row 37: St st   (18 sts)

Row 38 (Wrong side): K18   (18 sts)

Cut off the dark gray yarn, continue knitting with the light beige.

Row 39: K18   (18 sts)

Row 40 – Row 44: St st   (18 sts)

Row 45: K2tog x9   (9 sts)

Row 46: P9   (9 sts)

Row 47: K2tog x4, K1   (5 sts)

Leaving a long tail for sewing, then cut off the yarn.
Thread this tail through remaining stitches and pull up tightly. (Fig. 11)

Fig. 11

HEAD (Make 1)

Cast on 26 stitches in light beige.

Row 1: K26   (26 sts)

Row 2: P26   (26 sts)

Row 3 – Row 4: St st   (26 sts)

Row 5: K5, KRL, K2, KLL, K12, KRL, K2, KLL, K5   (30 sts)

Row 6 – Row 10: St st   (30 sts)

Row 11: K6, KRL, K2, KLL, K14, KRL, K2, KLL, K6   (34 sts)

Row 12: P34   (34 sts)

Using 2 ends of different color yarn to marker. (I've used red yarn to illustrate). Where 2 ends of the red yarn come out, we will attach the eyes to the head later.

Row 13: K15, place marker by one end of the red yarn *(Fig. 12)*, K4, place marker by the other end of the red yarn *(Fig. 13)*, K15 *(Fig. 14)* (34 sts)

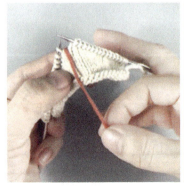

Fig. 12

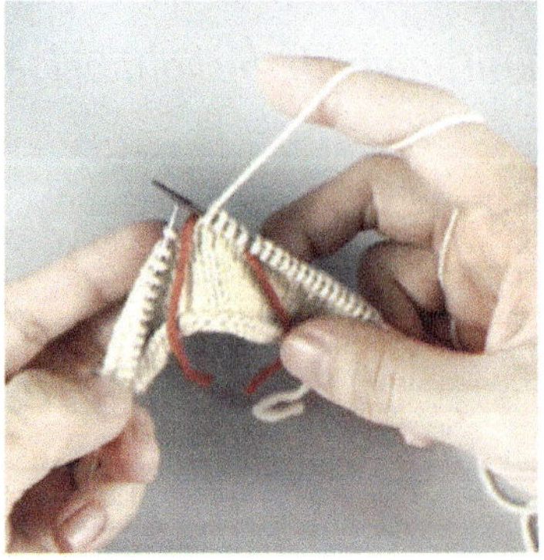

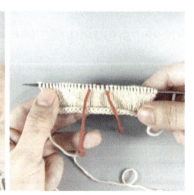

Fig. 13

Fig. 14

Row 14 – Row 20: St st   (34 sts)

Row 21: K7, KRL, K2, KLL, K16, KRL, K2, KLL, K7   (38 sts)

Row 22 – Row 28: St st   (38 sts)

Row 29: K8, KRL, K2, KLL, K18, KRL, K2, KLL, K8   (42 sts)

Row 30 – Row 42: St st   (42 sts)

Row 43: K6, SSK, K2tog, K5, SSK, K8, K2tog, K5, SSK, K2tog, K6   (36 sts)

Row 44: P36   (36 sts)

Row 45: K5, SSK, K2tog, K4, SSK, K6, K2tog, K4, SSK, K2tog, K5   (30 sts)

Row 46: P30   (30 sts)

Row 47: K4, SSK, K2tog, K3, SSK, K4, K2tog, K3, SSK, K2tog, K4   (24 sts)

Row 48: P30   (30 sts)

Row 49: K3, SSK, K2tog, K2, SSK, K2, K2tog, K2, SSK, K2tog, K3   (18 sts)

Row 50: Castt off.

Cut off the yarn.

ANTLERS (Make 1)

Cast on 6 stitches in brown.

Row 1: KFB x6   (12 sts)

Row 2: P12   (12 sts)

Row 3: K1, KFB x10, K1   (22 sts)

Row 4: P22   (22 sts)

Row 5 – Row 8: St st   (22 sts)

Row 9: SSK x2, K14, K2tog x2   (18 sts)

Row 10: P18   (18 sts)

Row 11: SSK x2, K10, K2tog x2   (14 sts)

Row 12: P14   (14 sts)

Row 13: SSK, K3, SSK, K2tog, K3, K2tog   (10 sts)

Row 14: P10   (10 sts)

Row 15: K10   (10 sts)

Row 16: P10   (10 sts)

Row 17: Cast on 3 stitches *(Fig. 15)*, K13, cast on 3 stitches *(Fig. 16)* (16 sts)

Row 18 – Row 20: St st (16 sts)

Row 21: Cast off 3 stitches, K12 (13 sts)

Row 22: Cast off 3 stitches, P9 *(Fig. 17)* (10 sts)

Fig. 15

Fig. 16

Fig. 17

Row 23 – Row 54: St st (10 sts)

Row 55: Cast on 3 stitches, K13, cast on 3 stitches (16 sts)

Row 56 – Row 58: St st (16 sts)

Row 59: Cast off 3 stitches, K12 (13 sts)

Row 60: Cast off 3 stitches, P9 (10 sts)

Row 61 – Row 64: St st (10 sts)

Row 65: K1, KRL, K3, KRL, K2, KLL, K3, KLL, K1 (14 sts)

Row 66: P14 (14 sts)

Row 67: [K1, KRL] x2, K10, [KLL, K1] x2 (18 sts)

Row 68: P18 (18 sts)

Row 69: [K1, KRL] x2, K14, [KLL, K1] x2 (22 sts)

Row 70 – Row 74: St st (22 sts)

Row 75: K1, K2tog x 10, K1 (12 sts)

Row 76: P12 (12 sts)

Row 77: K2tog x2 (6 sts)

Leaving a long tail for sewing, then cut off the yarn.
Thread this tail through remaining stitches and pull up tightly. (Fig. 18)

Fig. 18

EARS (Make 2)

Cast on 10 stitches in light beige, leaving a long tail for sewing.

Row 1: K10   (10 sts)

Row 2: P10   (10 sts)

Row 3 – Row 8: St st   (10 sts)

Row 9: K1, K2tog x4, K1   (6 sts)

Row 10: P6   (6 sts)

Row 11: K2tog x3   (3 sts)

Leaving a long tail for sewing, then cut off the yarn.
Thread this tail through remaining stitches and pull up tightly.

SHOES (Make 2)

Cast on 22 stitches in brown, leaving a long tail for sewing.

Row 1: K1, KFB, [K2, KFB] x3, [KFB, K2] x3, KFB, K1   (30 sts)

Row 2: P30   (30 sts)

Row 3: K2, KFB, [K3, KFB] x3, [KFB, K3] x3, KFB, K2   (38 sts)

Row 4: P38   (38 sts)

Row 5: K38   (38 sts)

Row 6 (Wrong side): K38   (38 sts)

Cut off the brown yarn, continue knitting with the light brown.

Row 7: K38   (38 sts)

Row 8: P38   (38 sts)

Row 9 (Right side): P38   (38 sts)

Row 10: P38   (38 sts)

Row 11: K14, SSK, K6, K2tog, K14   (36 sts)

Row 12: P36   (36 sts)

Row 13: K14, SSK, K4, K2tog, K14   (34 sts)

Row 14: P34   (34 sts)

Row 15: K14, SSK, K2, K2tog, K14   (32 sts)

Row 16: P32   (32 sts)

Row 17: K14, SSK, K2tog, K14   (30 sts)

Row 18: P30   (30 sts)

Row 19: K8, cast off 5 stitches *(Fig. 19)* (there should be left 16 stitches on the left needle to work), K2tog *(Fig. 20)*, then cast off this K2tog stitch, continue knitting and cast off next 7 stitches, K7 *(Fig. 21)* (16 sts)

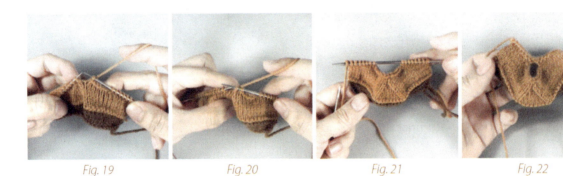

Fig. 19   *Fig. 20*   *Fig. 21*   *Fig. 22*

Row 20 (Wrong side): K16   (16 sts)

Row 21: Cast off

Leaving a long tail for sewing. Then, we'll cut off the yarn. (Fig. 22)

SHOE CUFFS (Make 2)

Cast on 30 stitches in brown, leaving a long tail for sewing.

Row 1: K30   (30 sts)

Row 2 – Row 9: St st   (30 sts)

Row 10: P28, P2tog   (29 sts)

Row 11: Cast off 7 stitches, K19, K2tog   (21 sts)

Row 12: Cast off 7 stitches (there should be left 13 stitches on the left needle to work), P13 (14 sts)

Row 13: K1, KRL, K12, KLL, K1 (16 sts)

Row 14 (Wrong side): K1, KRL, K14, KLL, K1 (18 sts)

Row 15: P18 (18 sts)

Row 16: K1, KRL, K16, KLL, K1 (20 sts)

Row 17: P20 (20 sts)

Row 18: K1, KRL, K18, KLL, K1 (22 sts)

Row 19: P22 (22 sts)

Row 20: K1, KRL, K20, KLL, K1 (24 sts)

Row 21: Cast off

Fig. 23

Cut off the yarn. (Fig. 23)

PANTS (Make 1)

Cast on 52 stitches in green, leaving a long tail for sewing.

Row 1: [K1, P1] x 26 (52 sts)

Row 2: [K1, P1] x 26 (52 sts)

Row 3: K2, [KRL, K12] x2, [K12, KLL] x2, K2 (56 sts)

Row 4: P56 (56 sts)

Row 5: K1, [KRL, K9] x3, [K9, KLL] x3, K1 (62 sts)

Row 6 – Row 12: St st (62 sts)

Row 13: K1, [KRL, K10] x3, [K10, KLL] x3, K1 (68 sts)

Row 14 – Row 18: St st (68 sts)

Row 19: K1, [KRL, K11] x3, [K11, KLL] x3, K1 (74 sts)

Row 20 – Row 24: St st (74 sts)

Row 25: K1, [KRL, K12] x3, [K12, KLL] x3, K1 (80 sts)

Row 26 – Row 40: St st (80 sts)

We have 80 stitches on the left needle. Transfer 40 stitches on the left to a holder to knit later. We'll start knitting 40 stitches on the right first.

The first pant leg:

Row 41: K1, SSK, K34, K2tog, K1 (38 sts)

Row 42: P38 (38 sts)

Row 43: K1, SSK, K32, K2tog, K1 (36 sts)

Row 44: P36 (36 sts)

Row 45: K1, SSK, K30, K2tog, K1 (34 sts)

Row 46: P34 (34 sts)

Row 47: K1, SSK, K28, K2tog, K1 (32 sts)

Row 48: P32 (32 sts)

Row 49: K1, SSK, K26, K2tog, K1 (30 sts)

Row 50: P30 (30 sts)

Row 51: K1, SSK, K24, K2tog, K1 (28 sts)

Row 52: P28 (28 sts)

Row 53 (Right side): P28 (28 sts)

Row 54: P28 (28 sts)

Row 55: K28 (28 sts)

Row 56: Cast off

Leaving a long tail for sewing. Then, we'll cut off the yarn.

The second pant leg:

Using the green yarn to knit (repeat the Row 41 – Row 56 of the first pants leg). (Fig. 24)

Fig. 24

COAT (Make 1)

Cast on 30 stitches in red.

Row 1: P30   (30 sts)

Row 2: P2, K4, yo, K1, yo, K3, yo, K1, yo, K8, yo, K1, yo, K3, yo, K1, yo, K4, P2   (38 sts)

Row 3: P38   (38 sts)

Row 4: P2, K5, yo, K1, yo, K5, yo, K1, yo, K10, yo, K1, yo, K5, yo, K1, yo, K5, P2   (46 sts)

Row 5: P46   (46 sts)

Row 6: P2, K6, yo, K1, yo, K7, yo, K1, yo, K12, yo, K1, yo, K7, yo, K1, yo, K6, P2   (54 sts)

Row 7: P54   (54 sts)

Row 8: P2, K7, yo, K1, yo, K9, yo, K1, yo, K14, yo, K1, yo, K9, yo, K1, yo, K7, P2   (62 sts)

Row 9: P62   (62 sts)

Row 10: P2, K8, yo, K1, yo, K11, yo, K1, yo, K16, yo, K1, yo, K11, yo, K1, yo, K8, P2   (70 sts)

Row 11: P70   (70 sts)

Row 12: P2, K9, yo, K1, yo, K1, P11, K1, yo, K1, yo, K18, yo, K1, yo, K1, P11, K1, yo, K1, yo, K9, P2 (78 sts)

Row 13: P78   (78 sts)

Row 14: P2, K10, yo, K1, yo, K15, yo, K1, yo, K20, yo, K1, yo, K15, yo, K1, yo, K10, P2   (86 sts)

Row 15 (Wrong side): K15, cast off 15 stitches, K25, cast off 15 stitches, K14 *(Fig. 25)*   (56 sts)

Row 16: P2, K13, cast on 4 stitches, K26, cast on 4 stitches, K13, P2 *(Fig. 26)*   (64 sts)

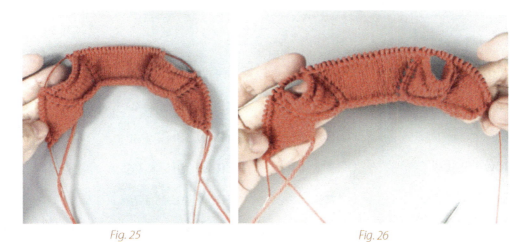

Fig. 25   *Fig. 26*

Row 17: P64   (64 sts)

Row 18: P2, K19, K2tog, K18, K2tog, K19, P2   (62 sts)

Row 19: P62   (62 sts)

Row 20: P2, K58, P2   (62 sts)

Row 21 – Row 28: Repeat Row 19 – Row 20 four times.

Row 29: P62   (62 sts)

Row 30 (Right side): P62   (62 sts)

Row 31: P2, K20, KRL, K18, KLL, K20, P2   (64 sts)

Row 32: P64   (64 sts)

Row 33: P64   (64 sts)

Row 34: P2, K60, P2   (64 sts)

Row 35 – Row 42: Repeat Row 33 – Row 34

Row 43: P64   (64 sts)

Row 44: P64   (64 sts)

Row 45 – Row 58: Repeat Row 33 – Row 34

Row 59: [K1, P1] x 32   (64 sts)

Row 60: [K1, P1] x 32   (64 sts)

Row 61: Cast off.

Cut off the yarn. *(Fig. 27)*

Fig. 27

TOGGLES / BUTTONHOLES (Make 4)

Cast on 14 stitches in light brown, leaving a long tail for sewing.

Cast off all stitches and cut off the yarn.

BAG (Make 1)

Cast on 12 stitches in brown.

Row 1: P12   (12 sts)

Row 2: K12   (12 sts)

Row 3 – Row 15: St st   (12 sts)

Row 16 (Right side): P12   (12 sts)

Row 17: K12   (12 sts)

Row 18: K12   (12 sts)

Row 19 – Row 33: Repeat Row 17 – Row 18

Row 34: P12   (12 sts)

Row 35: SSK, K10   (11 sts)

Row 36: P9, P2tog   (10 sts)

Row 37: SSK, K8   (9 sts)

Row 38: P7, P2tog   (8 sts)

Row 39: SSK, K6   (7 sts)

Row 40: P5, P2tog   (6 sts)

Row 41: SSK, K4   (5 sts)

Row 42: P3, P2tog   (4 sts)

Row 43: SSK, K2   (3 sts)

Row 44: Cast off.

Cut off the yarn.

BAG LID (Make 1)

Cast on 12 stitches in light brown.

Row 1: K12   (12 sts)

Row 2: P12   (12 sts)

Row 3 – Row 5: St st   (12 sts)

Row 6: Cast off.

Cut off the yarn.

BAG CORD (Make 1)

Cast on 70 stitches in brown.

Cast off all stitches and cut off the yarn.

SEWING & MAKING UP

*You can see the Tutorial videos of my knitting patterns on **Cheryx.com***

(Cheryx.com > Tips & Tutorials > Tutorial videos)

| HOME | PATTERNS | FREE PATTERNS | TIPS & TUTORIALS | FAQs | CONTATT |

Home > Tips & Tutorials

Toy making techniques

Tutorial videos

Needles & yarns

Seams & Finishing

Other

Christmas reindeer Christopher – Tutorial videos

This is the tutorial video of knitting pattern "The friendly reindeer Christopher"

Mr.Pumpkin – Tutorial videos

This is the tutorial video of knitting pattern "The midnight guest Mr.Pumpkin"

Wooden doll Pinocchio – Tutorial videos

These are the tutorial videos of knitting pattern "My wooden doll Pinocchio"

LEGS & BODY

We'll use Mattress stitch to sew from A to B. Then, sewing the second leg in the same way (from C to D) *(Fig. 28)*.

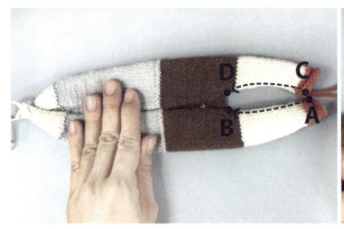

Fig. 28   *Fig. 29*

Now, it's time to stuff the legs *(Fig. 29)*. The easiest way to do this is breaking off two equally sized lumps of stuffing so that we will get both legs as the same size. Stuffing them so they are fairly firm but not straining the seams.

Then, using the tapestry needle to thread the cast on yarn, sewing 2 side edges together (sewing from E to F). *(Fig. 30)*

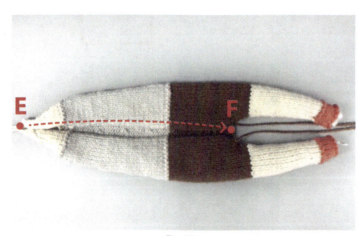

Fig. 30

Adding stuffing as you sew.

Make sure that you are satisfied with the stuffing then using the longest tail of one leg to sew the short edges between the legs. *(Fig. 31 - Fig. 35)*

Once finished, we'll tie off all of the tails and thread them through into the body to hide. *(Fig. 36)*

Fig. 31

Fig. 32

Fig. 33

Fig. 34

Fig. 35

Fig. 36

ARMS

We'll fold the arm and use the tapestry needle with cast off tail to sew the side edges together with help of the Mattress Stitch. Halfway along the seam stop and lightly stuff the arm, leaving the top of arm unstuffed so it stays floppy.

Continue sewing to the cast on edge, tie off 2 tails together. Repeat with the second arm.

HEAD

Attaching the beads that you planned to use as eyes to the place where we marked earlier (2 ends of red yarn) *(Fig. 37)*. Then secure it in place with the eye backs *(Fig. 38 - Fig. 39)*.

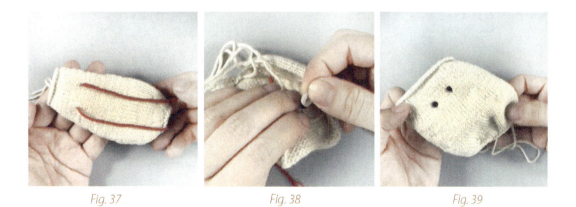

Fig. 37

Fig. 38

Fig. 39

We'll use Mattress stitch to sew from G to H *(Fig. 40)*. Adding stuffing as you sew.

Sewing the cast on edges *(Fig. 41 - Fig. 43)* and then, sewing cast off edges *(Fig. 44 - Fig. 45)*.

When finished, we will tie off all the tails together and poke them into body to hide. *(Fig. 46)*

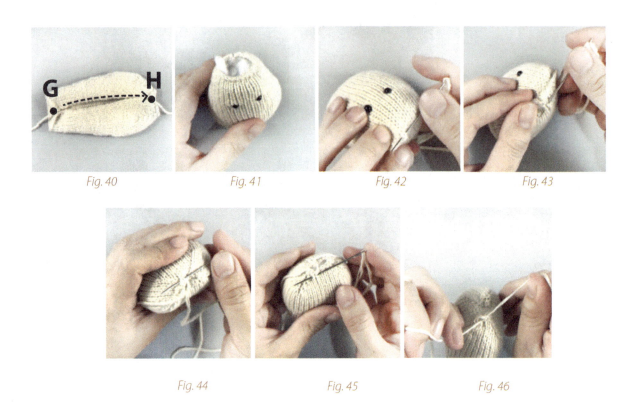

Fig. 40	Fig. 41	Fig. 42	Fig. 43

Fig. 44   Fig. 45   Fig. 46

ANTLERS

We'll use Whip stitch to sew the side edges together *(Fig. 47 - Fig.50)*. Adding stuffing (just a little) as you sew. *(Fig. 51)*

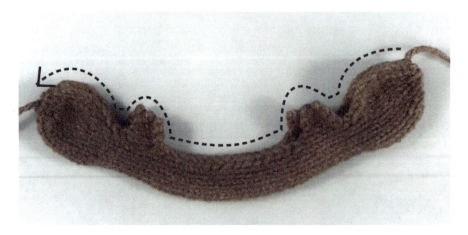

Fig. 47

Fig. 48   Fig. 49   Fig. 50   Fig. 51

Attach the antlers to the head *(Fig. 52)* for example as shown figure *(Fig. 53)*. (It is on the same horizontal as the eyes *(Fig. 54)*)

Fig. 52   Fig. 53   Fig. 54

EARS

Using the Whip Stitch on the side edge to transfer the cast off tail from I to J. *(Fig. 55 - Fig. 59)*

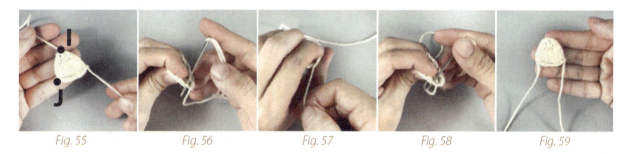

Fig. 55   Fig. 56   Fig. 57   Fig. 58   Fig. 59

We will fold the ears as shown in the figure *(Fig. 60 - Fig.61)* and use the sewing pins to adjust the ears to the head *(Fig. 62)*

Then using a long tail to attact them. After that, hiding all tails inside the head *(Fig. 63)* .

Fig. 60   Fig. 61   Fig. 62   Fig. 63

Using the ply of brown yarn to embroider the nose and make up the face. *(Fig. 64)*

It's time to attach the finished head to the finished body. We'll adjust the head with sewing pins to the body (L is middle K and M) *(Fig. 65 - Fig. 66)*.

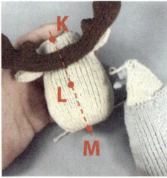

| Fig. 64 | Fig. 65 | Fig. 66 |

Thread the tapestry needle with one of the long tails from the neck and use it to sew the body and head together like: Sewing through a stitch of the head *(Fig. 67)* and then through a stitch on the cast off edge of the neck *(Fig. 68)*.

While attaching them, stuff the neck as tightly as you can *(Fig. 69)*, so that the head can stay up and not droop.

When finished, we will tie off all the tails together and poke them into body to hide. *(Fig. 70)*

| Fig. 67 | Fig. 68 | Fig. 69 | Fig. 70 |

ARMS

We will fold the arms of the reindeer and using the tapestry needle with cast off tail to sew the side edges together. Adding stuffing as you sew, leaving the top of arms unstuffed so it stays flopp.

Using the sewing pins to adjust the arms to the body and sewing them.

We will sew alternately through a stitch of shoulder and a stitch of the arm *(Fig. 72 - Fig. 73)*. Work all the way around the arm to join both the upper and the lower side *(Fig. 74 - Fig.76)*.

Fig. 71   Fig. 72   Fig. 73   Fig. 74

Fig. 75

COAT

We will fold the toggles *(Fig. 76)*. Then, sewing the buttons and toggles to the coat *(Fig. 77 - Fig.78)*.

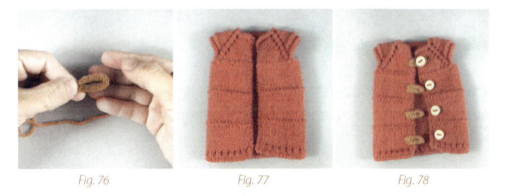

Fig. 76   Fig. 77   Fig. 78

PANTS

Using the long tail to sew 2 side edges together (sewing from N to O). Then, sewing from P to Q

(Fig. 79)

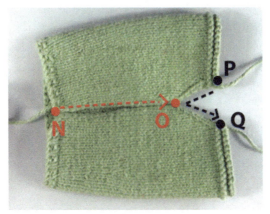

Fig. 79

SHOES

Using the cast on tail to sew the opening in the lower part of the shoes with Whip Stitch (Sewing from R to S) *(Fig. 80 - Fig. 83)*.

| *Fig. 80* | *Fig. 81* | *Fig. 82* | *Fig. 83* |

Then continue sewing from R to T with Mattress Stitch *(Fig. 80)*. Adding stuffing as you sew *(Fig. 84)*. Using a long tail to sew the opening in the upper part of the shoes with the Whip Stitch *(Fig. 85-Fig. 86)*

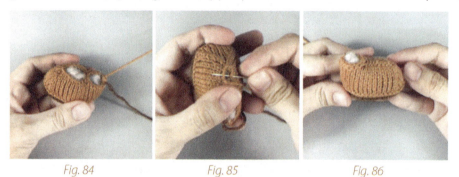

| *Fig. 84* | *Fig. 85* | *Fig. 86* |

We'll put on coat and pants for Christopher *(Fig. 87)* and use the long tails to attach the shoes to the legs (Sewing alternately through a stitch of leg and a stitch of the shoe *(Fig. 88 - Fig. 90)*).

Fig. 87

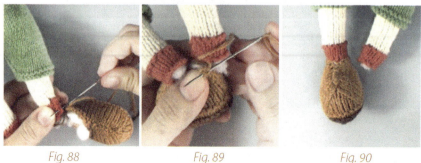

| *Fig. 88* | *Fig. 89* | *Fig. 90* |

We'll use the sewing pins to adjust the shoe cuffs to shoes *(Fig. 91)*. Then, using Whip stitches to attach them as shown in the figure *(Fig. 92 - Fig. 96)*

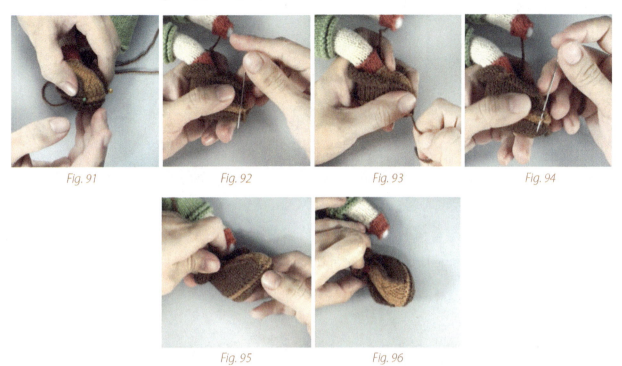

Fig. 91   Fig. 92   Fig. 93   Fig. 94

Fig. 95   Fig. 96

Using the sewing pins to adjust the shoe cuffs *(Fig. 97)*, then we'll use the light brown to make the shoelaces *(Fig. 98)*. Sewing the second shoes in the same way *(Fig. 99)*.

Fig. 97   Fig. 98   Fig. 99

BAG

We will fold the bag of as shown in the figure. *(Fig. 100)*

Using the Whip stitch to sew the side edges (from U to V, W to X) *(Fig. 101)*. Don't stuff the bag.

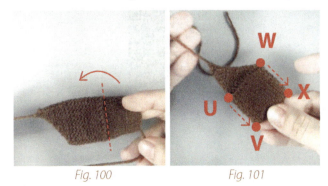

Fig. 100   Fig. 101

Sewing the bag lid to the bag. *(Fig. 102 - Fig. 104)*

Fig. 102   Fig. 103   Fig. 104

Then, using the brown yarn to make up the lid *(Fig. 105)*.

We'll sew the bag cord to the bag at Y and Z and then hide the tails *(Fig. 106)*.

Fig. 105   Fig. 106

Dear Customer

I am on emerging editor and, with the sales made by the book, I can continue my studies to publish other books on the subject. I would appreciate on honest review from you.

Also, please if you notice any mistakes or missing information, feel free to contact me at this e-mail address: wwwanacraft@gmail.com
Thank you for your support

Write to us to get extra free content for you

ENJOY SUMMER!

My friendly crocodile

Alan

— Pattern by Cheryx —

NEEDLES

- Two pairs of 2.25mm (US 1) straight needles

MATERIALS

- Toy stuffing (less than 50g)
- Tapestry needle
- Sewing pins
- 2 beads - for the eyes (8 mm)
- Holder needle

YARNS

Less than 50g in each colour:

- Jeans - Yarn Art

   Yellow 84

  White 01

  Black 28

- Susan

  Green 32

  Brown 26

- Gazzal Baby Cotton

  Red 3453

NOTES

- **Finished size:** The finished toy is 25cm tall

- **Gauge:** 26 sts and 34 rows = 4" [10 cm] in Stockinette Stitch . Don't worry too much about tension for this pattern.

- **Work flat:** All pieces are knitted flat

- **Casting on:** Unless otherwise specified, I prefer to use the long tail cast on for all pieces.

- **Sewing seams:** Use Mattress Stitch and Whip Stitch to sew the seams.

- **Safety:** If you are making these toys to give to a child, please consider your choice of toy eyes carefully, and ensure you have no loose parts (loose threads, buttons, etc) which can be potential.

ABBREVIATIONS

K	Knit	**RS**	Right side
P	Purl	**WS**	Wrong side
Kfb	*Increase:* Knit into the front and back of the next stitch	**st(s)**	Stitch(es)

K2tog   *Decrease:* Knit two stitches together

K3tog   *Decrease:* Knit three stitches together

SSK   *Decrease:* Slip a stitch (as if to knit it) to the right-hand needle, slip a second stitch in the same way, slip both stitches together back to the left-hand needle and knit together through the back loops.

Stocking Stitch (St st)
Knit all stitches on right side rows, purl all stitches on wrong side rows

(.. sts)   The number in round brackets at the end of the instruction indicates the number of stitches after working the row.

[...]   Repeat the sequence between the square brackets by the number indicated.

KNITTING PATTERN OF ALAN

LEGS

The first leg

Cast on 10 stitches in green yarn, leaving a long tail for sewing.

Row 1 (WS): P10   (10)

Row 2 (RS): KFB x 10   (20)

Row 3: P20   (20)

Row 4: K1, [K2, KFB] x6, K1   (26)

Row 5 – Row 21: St St   (26)

Cut off the green yarn , continue knitting with the red yarn.

Row 22: K26   (26)

Row 23 (WS): K26   (26)

Row 24: K1, [K5, KFB] x4, K1   (30)

Row 25: P30   (30)

Row 26 – Row 31: St St   (30)

Fig. 1

Cut off the yarn. (Fig. 1)

Now, we are having 30 stitches and we will continue knitting it later , so we can put the first leg to one side. (If you don't have enough knitting needles, you can transfer 30 stitches into a cable needle or holder needle.)

The second leg

Row 1 – Row 31: *Repeat* **Row 1 – Row 31** *of the first leg. But don't cut off the yarn, we will use this yarn to continue knitting the body.*

Row 32: Cast on 3 stitches *(Fig. 2)*, K33 *(Fig. 3)*, cast on 5 stitches, *(continue knitting 30 stitches of the first leg)* K30 *(Fig. 4)*, cast on 3 stitches *(Fig. 5)* (71)

Fig. 2

Fig. 3

Fig. 4

Fig. 5

Continue knitting the next row to make the body.

BODY

Row 33 – Row 37: St St   (71)

Row 38: K1, [K10, KFB] x3, K3, [KFB, K10] x3, K1   (77)

Row 39 – Row 43: St St   (77)

Row 44: K1, [K15, KFB] x2, K11, [KFB, K15] x2, K1 (81)

Row 45 – Row 53: St St   (81)

Row 54: K3, [K2tog, K13] x5, K3   (76)

Row 55 – Row 57: St St   (76)

Row 58: K2, [K10, K2tog] x6, K2   (70)

Row 59 – Row 61: St St   (70)

Row 62: K2, [K9, K2tog] x6, K2   (64)

Row 63: P64   (64)

Cut off the red yarn , continue knitting with the white yarn.

Row 64: K64   (64)

Row 65 (WS): K64   (64)

Row 66: K64   (64)

Row 67: P64   (64)

Row 68: K2, [K8, K2tog] x6, K2   (58)

Row 69 (WS): K58   (58)

Cut off the white yarn , continue knitting with the green yarn.

Row 70: K58   (58)

Row 71: P58   (58)

Row 72: K2, [K7, K2tog] x6, K2   (52)

Row 73 – Row 81: St St   (52)

Row 82: K2, [K6, K2tog] x6, K2   (46)

Row 83 – Row 91: St St   (46)

Row 92: K2, [K5, K2tog] x6, K2   (40)

Row 93 – Row 99: St St   (40)

Row 100: K2, [K4, K2tog] x6, K2   (34)

Row 101: P34   (34)

Row 102: Cast off

Leaving a long tail for sewing.

Then cut off the yarn. (Fig. 6)

Fig. 6

TAIL (Make 1)

Cast on 44 stitches in green, leaving a long tail for sewing.

Row 1: P44	(44)	**Row 20:** K13, SSK, K2tog, K13	(28)
Row 2: KFB, K19, K3tog, K20, KFB	(44)	**Row 21:** P28	(28)
Row 3: P44	(44)	**Row 22:** K12, SSK, K2tog, K12	(26)
Row 4: K1, KFB, K16, SSK x2, K2tog x2, K16, KFB, K1	(42)	**Row 23 – Row 25:** St St	(26)
		Row 26: K9, K2tog, K4, K2tog, K9	(24)
Row 5: P42	(42)	**Row 27 – Row 29:** St St	(24)
Row 6: K1, KFB, K17, SSK, K2tog, K17, KFB, K1	(42)	**Row 30:** K8, K2tog, K4, K2tog, K8	(22)
		Row 31 – Row 33: St St	(22)
Row 7: P42	(42)	**Row 34:** K7, K2tog, K4, K2tog, K7	(20)
Row 8: K19, SSK, K2tog, K19	(40)	**Row 35 – Row 37:** St St	(20)
Row 9: P40	(40)	**Row 38:** K6, K2tog, K4, K2tog, K6	(18)
Row 10: K18, SSK, K2tog, K18	(38)	**Row 39 – Row 41:** St St	(18)
Row 11: P38	(38)	**Row 42:** K5, K2tog, K4, K2tog, K5	(16)
Row 12: K17, SSK, K2tog, K17	(36)	**Row 43 – Row 45:** St St	(16)
Row 13: P36	(36)	**Row 46:** K4, K2tog, K4, K2tog, K4	(14)
Row 14: K16, SSK, K2tog, K16	(34)	**Row 47 – Row 49:** St S	(14)
Row 15: P34	(34)	**Row 50:** K3, K2tog, K4, K2tog, K3	(12)
Row 16: K15, SSK, K2tpg, K15	(32)	**Row 51 – Row 53:** St St	(12)
Row 17: P32	(32)	**Row 54:** K2, K2tog, K4, K2tog, K2	(10)
Row 18: K14, SSK, K2tog, K14	(30)	**Row 55 – Row 57:** St St	(10)
Row 19: P30	(30)	**Row 58:** K1, K2tog, K4, K2tog, K1	(8)

Leaving a long tail for sewing, then cut off the yarn.

Thread this tail through remaining stitches and pull up tightly. (Fig. 7)

Fig. 7

HEAD (Make 1)

Cast on 8 stitches in green, leaving a long tail for sewing.

Row 1: KFB x8   (16)

Row 2: P16   (16)

Row 3: K1, [K1, KFB] x7, K1   (23)

Row 4: P23   (23)

Row 5: K1, [K2, KFB] X7, K1   (30)

Row 6: P30   (30)

Row 7: K1, [K3, KFB] X7, K1   (37)

Row 8: P37   (37)

Row 9: K1, [K4, KFB] X7, K1   (44)

Row 10: P44   (44)

Row 11: K1, [K5, KFB] X7, K1   (51)

Row 12: P51   (51)

Row 13: K1, [K6, KFB] X7, K1   (58)

Row 14 – Row 30: St St   (58)

Row 31: K1, K2tog, K10, [K2tog, K8] x4, K2, K2tog, K1 (52)

Row 32 – Row 36: St St   (52)

Row 37: K1, K2tog, K10, [K2tog, K6] x4, K4, K2tog, K1 (46)

Row 38: P46   (46)

Row 39: K17, P12, K17   (46)

Row 40: P46   (46)

Row 41: K1, K2tog, K7, [K2tog, K6] x4, K1, K2tog, K1 (40)

Row 42: P40   (40)

Row 43: K14, P12, K14   (40)

Row 44: P40   (40)

Row 45: K1, K2tog, K7, [K2tog, K4] x4, K3, K2tog, K1 (34)

Row 46: P34   (34)

Row 47: K12, P10, K12   (34)

Row 48 – Row 50: St St   (34)

Row 51: K12, P10, K12   (34)

Row 52 – Row 58: St St   (34)

Row 59: K1, K2tog, K4, [K2tog, K4] x4, K2tog, K1 (28)

Row 60 – Row 64: St St   (28)

Row 65: Cast off

Leaving a long tail for sewing. Then cut off the yarn.

NOSTRILS (Make 2)

Cast on 5 stitches in green, leaving a long tail for sewing.

Row 1: K5   (5)

Leaving a long tail for sewing, then cut off the yarn.
Thread this tail through remaining stitches and pull up tightly.

EYES (Make 2)

Cast on 6 stitches in green, leaving a long tail for sewing.

Row 1: KFB x6   (12)

Row 2: P12   (12)

Row 3: [K1, KFB] x6   (18)

Row 4: P18 (18)

Row 5: [K2, KFB] x6 (24)

Row 6 – Row 9: St St (24)

Row 10 (WS): K24 (24)

Cut off the green yarn , continue knitting with the white yarn.

Row 11: [K2, K2tog] x6 (18)

Row 12: P18 (18)

Row 13: [K1, K2tog] x6 (12)

Row 14: P12 (12)

Row 15: K2tog x6 (6)

Leaving a long tail for sewing, then cut off the yarn. Thread this tail through remaining stitches and pull up tightly. (Fig. 8)

Fig. 8

ARMS (Make 2)

Cast on 10 stitches in green, leaving a long tail for sewing.

Row 1: K1, [K1, KFB] x4, K1 (14)

Row 2: P14 (14)

Row 3: K1, [K1, KFB] x6, K1 (20)

Row 4 - Row 12: St St (20)

Row 13: K1, [K7, K2tog] x2, K1 (18)

Row 14 – Row 34: St St (18)

Row 35: K1, K2tog, K12, K2tog, K1 (16)

Row 36 – Row 40: St St (16)

Row 41: K1, K2tog, K10, K2tog, K1 (14)

Row 42: P14 (14)

Row 43: Cast off

Leaving a long tail for sewing. Then cut off the yarn. (Fig. 9)

Fig. 9

SEWING & MAKING UP

SEWING THE LEGS

Thread the tapestry needle with cast on long tail through the loops of the cast on stitches of leg (10 sts) and pull up tightly (*I've used white yarn to illustrate*). *(Fig. 10 - FIg. 16)*

Fig. 10   Fig. 11   Fig. 12

Fig. 13   Fig. 14   Fig. 15

Then using Mattress Stitch to sew from A to B.

Fig. 16

Sew the second leg in the same way.

Now, it's time to stuff the legs. The easiest way to do this is breaking off two equally sized lumps of stuffing so that we will get both legs as the same size. Stuffing them so they are fairly firm but not straining the seams. *(Fig.17)*

Fig. 17

SEWING THE BODY

Then using Mattress Stitch to sew from C to D *(Fig.18)*.

Adding stuffing as you sew, stuff them so they are fairly firm but not straining the seams. Then continue sewing the back of the body *(Fig.19)*.

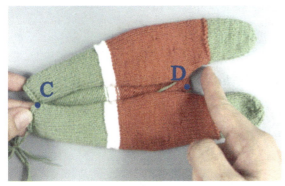

Fig. 18

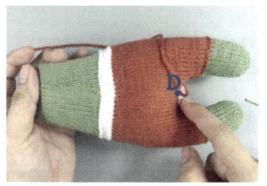

Fig. 19

Make sure that you are satisfied with the stuffing then sew the short edges between the legs with the Mattress stitch. Using the longest tail of legs to sew *(I've used white yarn to illustrate)* *(Fig.21 - Fig. 21)*. Once finished, tie all of the tails of the legs and thread them through into the body to hide.

Fig. 20

Fig. 21

SEWING THE TAIL

Using Mattress Stitch to sew from E to F.

Adding stuffing as you sew, stuff them so they are fairly firm but not straining the seams. Then continue sewing the back of the body *(Fig.22 - Fig.23)*.

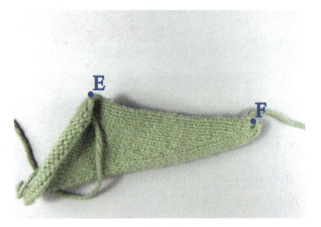

Fig. 22   *Fig. 23*

ATTACH THE TAIL TO THE BODY

Tutorial Video "How to attach the tail to the body": https://youtu.be/Qt7l1_lsJTw

Adjust the tail with sewing pins to the body *(Fig.24 - Fig.25)*.

Fig. 24   *Fig. 25*

To attach the tail, using the cast on tail of the finished tail to sew it in place. We will sew alternately through a stitch of body and a stitch of the tail as in the photos *(Fig.26 - Fig.30)*. Work all the way around the tail *(I've used white yarn to illustrate)*.

Fig. 26   *Fig. 27*   *Fig. 28*

Fig. 29   *Fig. 30*

Once it is attached, we will tie off all the tails together and we will poke them into the body to hide *(Fig.31 - Fig.32)*.

Fig. 31   *Fig. 32*

SEWING THE HEAD

Using a tapestry needle with cast on tail of the head, we'll pick up the loops from the cast on edge *(I've used white yarn to illustrate)* *(Fig.33 - Fig.34)* .

Then we will pull up tightly *(Fig.35)* continue sewing the side edges together. Adding stuffing as you sew, stuff them so they are fairly firm but not straining the seams *(Fig.36)*.

After that, tie off 2 long tails together *(Fig.37 - Fig.38)*.

Fig. 33   Fig. 34   Fig. 35

Fig. 36   Fig. 37   Fig. 38

Using Mattress Stitch to sew from G to H *(I've used white yarn to illustrate)* *(Fig.39 - Fig.41)*.

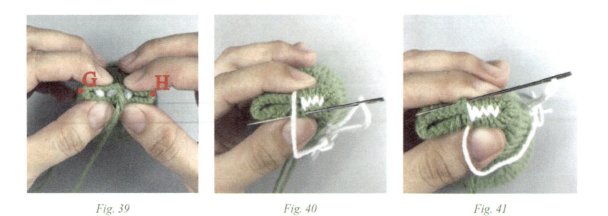

Fig. 39   Fig. 40   Fig. 41

Adding stuffing as you sew, stuff them so they are fairly firm but not straining the seams

Once finished, we'll tie off all the tails and poke them into the head to hide *(Fig.42 - Fig.43)*.

Fig. 42   Fig. 43

SEWING THE EYES

Using a tapestry needle with cast off tail to sew the side edges together with help of the Mattress Stitch.

Halfway along the seam, we'll stop.

If you use the toy eyes with thread end and washer buckle (plastic washers) *(Fig.44)* , we'll attach them to the eyes of Alan before you've finished the seam .

Attaching the beads that you planned to use as eyes. Then secure it in place with the eye backs *(Fig.45 - Fig.47)* .

Fig. 44   Fig. 45   Fig. 46   Fig. 47

Adding stuffing then continue sewing the side edges to the cast on edge *(Fig.48)*. After that, we'll pick up the loops from the cast on stitches and pull up tightly.

Once finished, tie off all the tails and poke them into the head to hide *(Fig.49)*.

Fig. 48   *Fig. 49*

ATTACH THE EYES TO THE HEAD

Adjust the eyes with sewing pins to the head as in the photos.*(J is middle I and K)*(Fig.50 - Fig. 51)

Fig. 50   *Fig. 51*

Thread the tapestry needle with one of the long tails from the eye and use it to sew the eye and head together. We will sew alternately through a stitch on the underside of the eye *(Fig.52)* and then through a stitch on the head *(Fig.53)*. Work around the underside of the eye in a circle.

Then we will tie off all the tails together and poke them into body to hide.

Fig. 52   *Fig. 53*

ATTACH THE NOSTRILS TO THE HEAD

Fix the nostrils with sewing pins to the head as in the photos *(Fig.54)*.

Thread the tapestry needle with one of the long tails from the nostril and use it to sew the nostril and head *(Fig.55 - Fig. 57)*.

Then we will tie off all the tails together and poke them into body to hide *(Fig.58)*.

Sewing the second nostril as the same way*(Fig.59)*.

| Fig. 54 | Fig. 55 | Fig. 56 |

| Fig. 57 | Fig. 58 | Fig. 59 |

ATTACH THE HEAD TO THE BODY

Fix the head with sewing pins to the body *(Fig.60)*.

Thread the tapestry needle with one of the long tails from the neck and use it to sew the body and head together. We will sew alternately through a stitch on the neck *(Fig.61)* and then through a stitch on the underside of the head *(Fig.62)*. Work around the underside of the head in a circle.

While attaching the head to the body, stuff the neck as tightly as you can *(Fig.63)*, so the head can stay up and not droop then continue sewing and go on stuffing the neck till it is very taut.

Then we will tie off all the tails together and poke them into body to hide *(Fig.64)*.

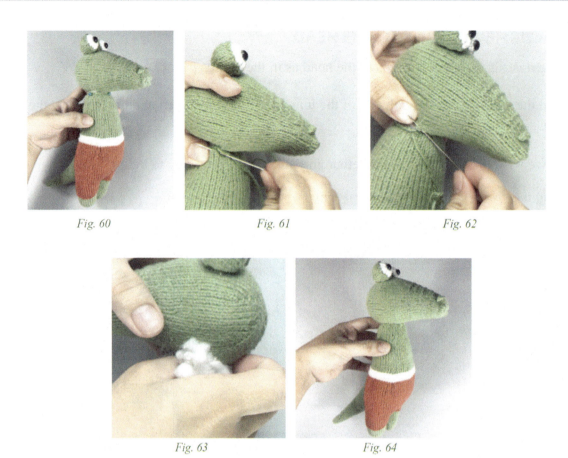

Fig. 60   Fig. 61   Fig. 62

Fig. 63   Fig. 64

SEWING THE ARMS

Fold the arms and using Whip Stitch to sew from L to M *(Fig.65)* *(I've used white yarn to illustrate)* *(Fig.66)*, then using Mattresss Stitch to sew from M to N.

Adding stuffing as you sew , leaving the top of arm unstuffed so it stays floppy, stuff them so that they are fairly firm but not straining the seams. Continue sewing to the cast off edge, tie off 2 tails together *(Fig.67)*.

Fig. 65   Fig. 66   Fig. 67

ATTACT THE ARMS TO THE BODY

Adjust the arms with sewing pins to the body *(Fig.68)*.

To attach the first arm, using the cast off tail from the top of the finished arm to sew it in place. We will sew alternately through a stitch of shoulder *(Fig.69)* and a stitch of the arm *(Fig.70) (I've used white yarn to illustrate)*. Work all the way around the arm to join both the upper and the lower side.

Once it is attached, tie off all the tails together and we will poke them into body to hide. Repeat with the second arm *(Fig.71)*.

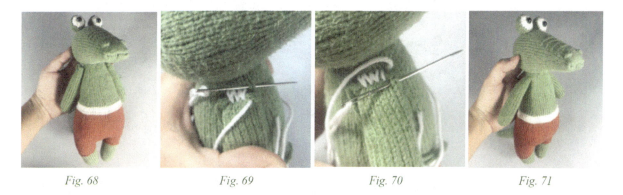

Fig. 68	*Fig. 69*	*Fig. 70*	*Fig. 71*

MAKING UP THE TROUSERS

To make the string on the trousers, we will use the tapestry needle with the red yarn to poke into the body at O and get the needle out in P *(Fig.72 - Fig.74)*.

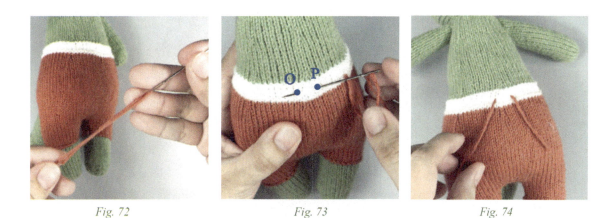

Fig. 72	*Fig. 73*	*Fig. 74*

We will tie a knot in the end of the yarn *(Fig.75)*, then cut off the yarn *(Fig76)*. Repeat with the other end of the yarn *(Fig.77 - Fig 78)*.

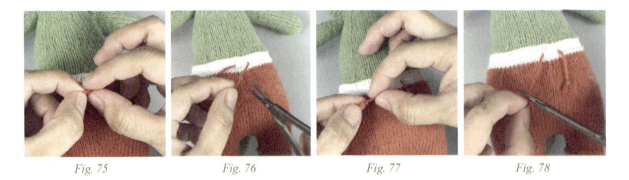

Fig. 75	*Fig. 76*	*Fig. 77*	*Fig. 78*

Then we will use the tapestry needle with the white yarn to making up the trousers as in the photos *(Fig 79 - Fig. 87)*.

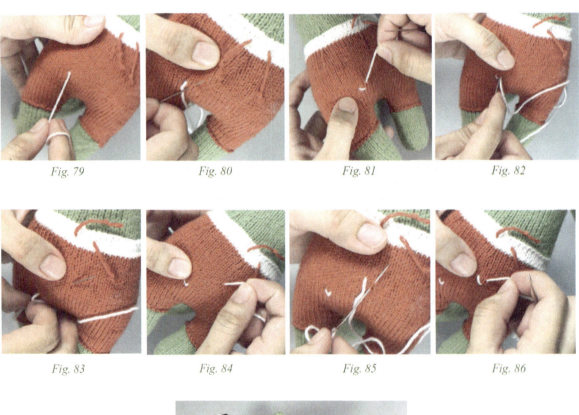

Fig. 79	*Fig. 80*	*Fig. 81*	*Fig. 82*

Fig. 83	*Fig. 84*	*Fig. 85*	*Fig. 86*

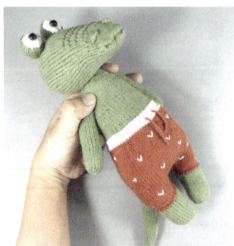

Fig. 87

KNITTING PATTERN OF THE DUCK FLOAT

FLOAT (Make 1)

*Cast on 73 stitches in yellow, leaving
a long tail for sewing.*

Row 1: K73	(73)	**Row 17:** K1, [K2tog, K13] x8	(113)
Row 2: P73	(73)	**Row 18:** P113	(113)
Row 3: K1, [KFB, K8] x8	(81)	**Row 19:** K1, [K2tog, K12] x8	(105)
Row 4: P81	(81)	**Row 20:** P105	(105)
Row 5: K1, [KFB, K9] x8	(89)	**Row 21:** K1, [K2tog, K11] x8	(97)
Row 6: P89	(89)	**Row 22:** P97	(97)
Row 7: K1, [KFB, K10] x8	(97)	**Row 23:** K1, [K2tog, K10] x8	(89)
Row 8: P97	(97)	**Row 24:** P89	(89)
Row 9: K1, [KFB, K11] x8	(105)	**Row 25:** K1, [K2tog, K9] x8	(81)
Row 10: P105	(105)	**Row 26:** P81	(81)
Row 11: K1, [KFB, K12] x8	(113)	**Row 27:** K1, [K2tog, K8] x8	(73)
Row 12: P113	(113)	**Row 28:** P73	(73)
Row 13: K1, [KFB, K13] x8	(121)	**Row 29:** Cast off.	
Row 14 – Row 16: St St	(121)		

*Leaving a long tail for sewing. Then cut
off the yarn.*

DUCK HEAD (Make 1)

Cast on 10 stitches in yellow, leaving a long tail for sewing.

Row 1: KFB x10	(20)
Row 2: P20	(20)
Row 3: K1, [KFB, K1] x9, K1	(29)
Row 4: P29	(29)
Row 5: K1, [KFB, K2] x9, K1	(38)
Row 6 – Row 14: St St	(38)
Row 15: K1, [K2tog, K2] x9, K2	(29)
Row 16: P29	(29)
Row 17: K1, [K2tog, K1] x9, K1	(20)
Row 18: P20	(20)
Row 19: K2tog x 10	(10)

*Leaving a long tail for sewing, then cut off the yarn. Thread this tail through remaining
stitches and pull up tightly.*

DUCK BEAK (Make 1)

Cast on 12 stitches in brown, leaving a long tail for sewing.

Row 1: K12　　　(12)

Row 2: P12　　　(12)

Row 3: Cast off

Leaving a long tail for sewing. Then cut off the yarn.

SEWING & MAKING UP THE DUCK FLOAT

SEWING THE FLOAT

Using a tapestry needle with the long tail to sew the cast on edge and the cast off edge together with help of the Mattress Stitch. Adding stuffing as you sew *(Fig. 88 - Fig.89)*. Then we will continue sewing the side edges together. When finished, we will tie off all the tails together ad poke them into the body to hide. *(Fig. 90)*

Fig. 88

Fig. 89

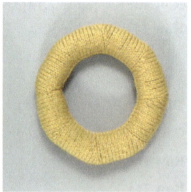

Fig. 90

SEWING THE DUCK HEAD

Using a tapestry needle with cast off tail of the head, we'll pull up tightly and sew the side edges together. Adding stuffing as you sew then continue sewing to the cast on edge *(Fig. 91)*

Fig. 91

ATTACH THE DUCK HEAD TO THE FLOAT

Thread the tapestry needle with one of the long tails from the duck head and use it to sew the head and float together. We will sew alternately through a stitch on the float*(Fig. 92)* and then through a stitch on the underside of the head *(Fig. 93)*.

While attaching the head to the body, adding stuffing the neck as tightly as you can *(Fig. 94)*.

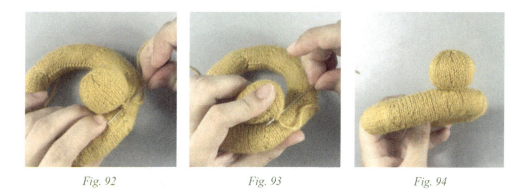

Fig. 92   Fig. 93   Fig. 94

ATTACH THE DUCK BEAK TO THE HEAD

Thread the tapestry needle with one of the long tails to sew the side edges of the beak together. Then using this tail to sew the beak and head together. We will sew alternately through a stitch on the beak and then through a stitch on the head *(Fig. 95 - Fig.97)*.

Work all the way around the beak to attach both the upper and the lower side.

Fig. 95   Fig. 96   Fig. 97

Then using the Whip Stitch to sew form Q to R *(Fig. 98- Fig.101)*.

Fig. 98   Fig. 99   Fig. 100   Fig. 101

EMBROIDER THE EYES

Thread the tapestry needle with black yarn to embroider the duck eyes as in the photos *(Fig. 102 - Fig.106)*.

Fig. 102

Fig. 103

Fig. 104

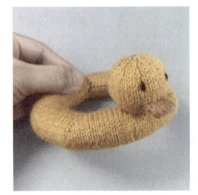
Fig. 105

Fig. 106

KNITTING PATTERN OF THE SUNGLASSES

SUNGLASSES (Make 2)

Cast on 24 stitches in black, leaving a long tail for sewing.

Row 1: K24   (24)

Row 2: P24   (24)

We'll have 24 stitches. Now we will transfer 12 stitches on the left to a holder to knit later (Fig. 107).

Countinue knitting 12 stitches on the right first:

Row 3: SSK, K8, K2tog   (10)

Row 4: P10   (10)

Row 5: SSK, K6, K2tog   (8)

Row 6: P8   (8)

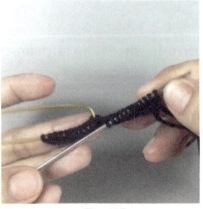
Fig. 107

Row 7: SSK, K4, K2tog   (6)

Row 8: P6   (6)

Row 9: Cast off *(Fig. 108)*.

Transfer 12 stitches on the holder to knitting needle. Now, we will knit remaining 12 stitches: repeat **Row 3 – Row 9**.

Make 2 the sunglasses (Fig. 109).

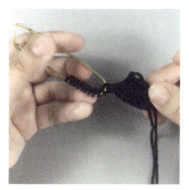 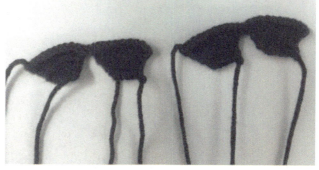

Fig. 108   Fig. 109

SEWING THE SUNGLASSES

Thread the tapestry needle with a cast on tail to sew the sunglasses.

Touch the two wrong sides of two sunglasses together then using the Whip Stitch to sew around the sunglasses to join them together *(Fig.110 - Fig.113)*.

Fig. 110   Fig. 111   Fig. 112

Fig. 113

Fix the sunglasses with sewing pins to the head.

We will attach the sunglasses to the head: Using the tapestry needle with the long tails S *(Fig.114)* to sew from S to T: We will sew alternately through a stitch on the sunglasses and then through a stitch on the head.

Then we will tie the long tail S and T together, poke them inside the body to hide.

Repeat with the long tail U and V.

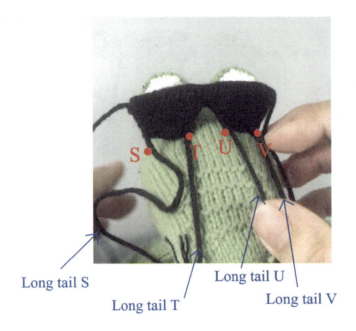

Fig. 114

Then using alternately the tapestry needle with the long tails X, Y *(Fig.115 - Fig.118)*:

- Poking the long tail X go inside the head in X and get out in Z
- Poking the long tail Y go inside the head in Y and get out in Z

Then we will tie long tails together, and poke them inside the body to hide.

Fig. 115   *Fig. 116*   *Fig. 117*   *Fig. 118*

Made in the USA
Las Vegas, NV
02 April 2025

20445313R00044